Blastoff! Readers are carefully developed by literacy experts to build reading stamina and move students toward fluency by combining standards-based content with developmentally appropriate text.

LEVELS

Level 1 provides the most support through repetition of high-frequency words, light text, predictable sentence patterns, and strong visual support.

Level 2 offers early readers a bit more challenge through varied sentences, increased text load, and text-supportive special features.

Level 3 advances early-fluent readers toward fluency through increased text load, less reliance on photos, advancing concepts, longer sentences, and more complex special features.

★ **Blastoff! Universe**

Reading Level

Grade K

Grades 1–3

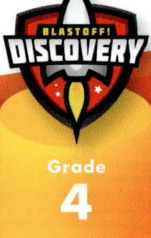
Grade 4

This edition first published in 2025 by Bellwether Media, Inc.

No part of this publication may be reproduced in whole or in part without written permission of the publisher. For information regarding permission, write to Bellwether Media, Inc., Attention: Permissions Department, 6012 Blue Circle Drive, Minnetonka, MN 55343.

Library of Congress Cataloging-in-Publication Data

Names: Langdo, Bryan, author.
Title: The Netherlands / by Bryan Langdo.
Description: Minneapolis , MN: Bellwether Media, Inc., 2025. | Series: Blastoff! Readers: Countries of the World | Includes bibliographical references and index. | Audience: Ages 5-8 | Audience: Grades 2-3 | Summary: "Relevant images match informative text in this introduction to the Netherlands. Intended for students in kindergarten through third grade"– Provided by publisher.
Identifiers: LCCN 2024039287 (print) | LCCN 2024039288 (ebook) | ISBN 9798893042306 (library binding) | ISBN 9798893043273 (ebook)
Subjects: LCSH: Netherlands–Juvenile literature.
Classification: LCC DJ18 .L36 2025 (print) | LCC DJ18 (ebook) | DDC 949.2–dc23/eng/20240830
LC record available at https://lccn.loc.gov/2024039287
LC ebook record available at https://lccn.loc.gov/2024039288

Text copyright © 2025 by Bellwether Media, Inc. BLASTOFF! READERS and associated logos are trademarks and/or registered trademarks of Bellwether Media, Inc.

Editor: Suzane Nguyen   Designer: Laura Sowers

Printed in the United States of America, North Mankato, MN.

Table of Contents

All About the Netherlands	4
Land and Animals	6
Life in the Netherlands	12
Netherlands Facts	20
Glossary	22
To Learn More	23
Index	24

All About the Netherlands

Amsterdam

The Netherlands is a small country in northwestern Europe. Its capital is Amsterdam.

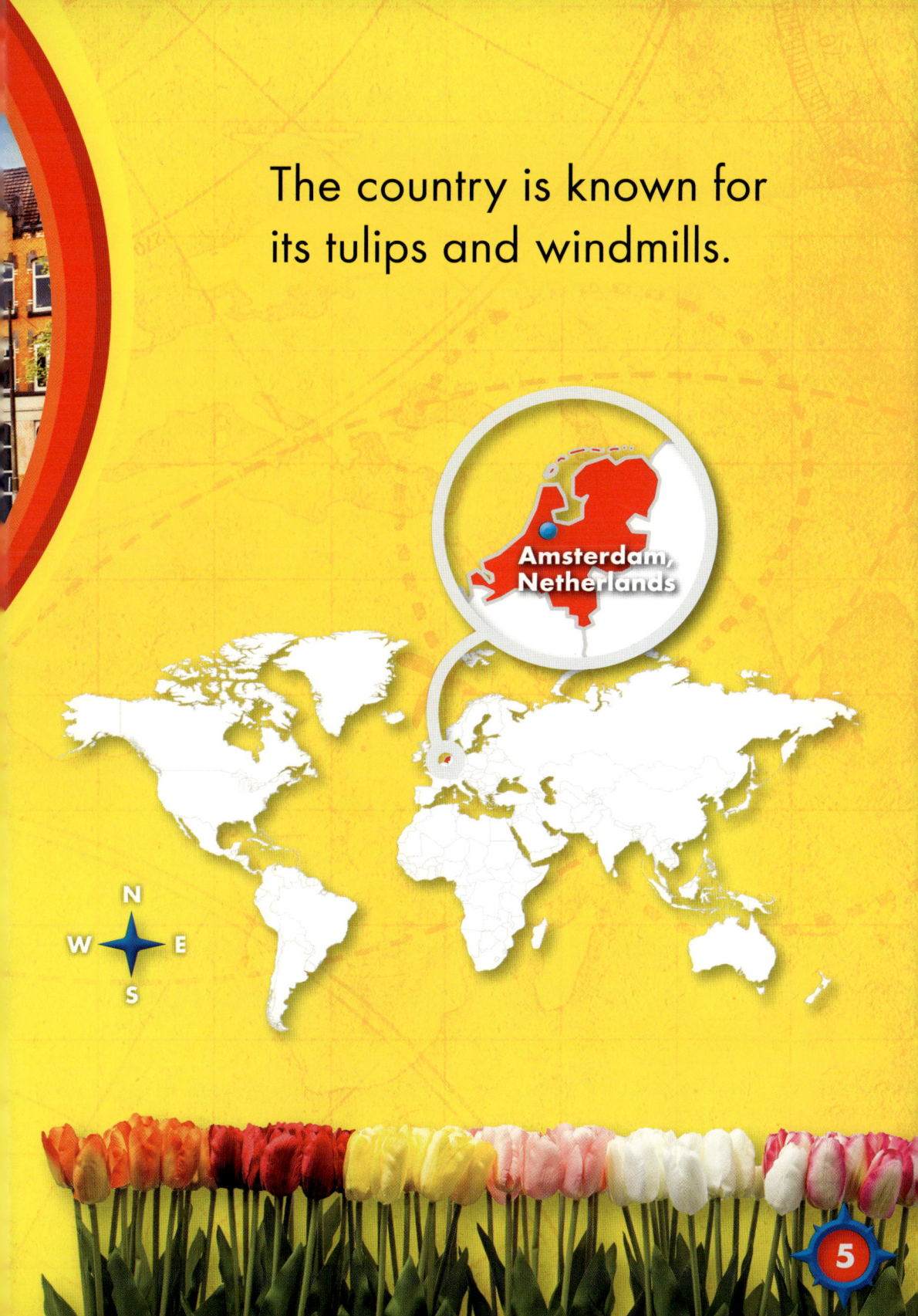

The country is known for its tulips and windmills.

Land and Animals

The Netherlands is mostly flat and low. **Canals**, dams, and **dikes** stop flooding. Sand and mud flats line the northern coast.

Rolling **plains** sit in the southeast.

dike

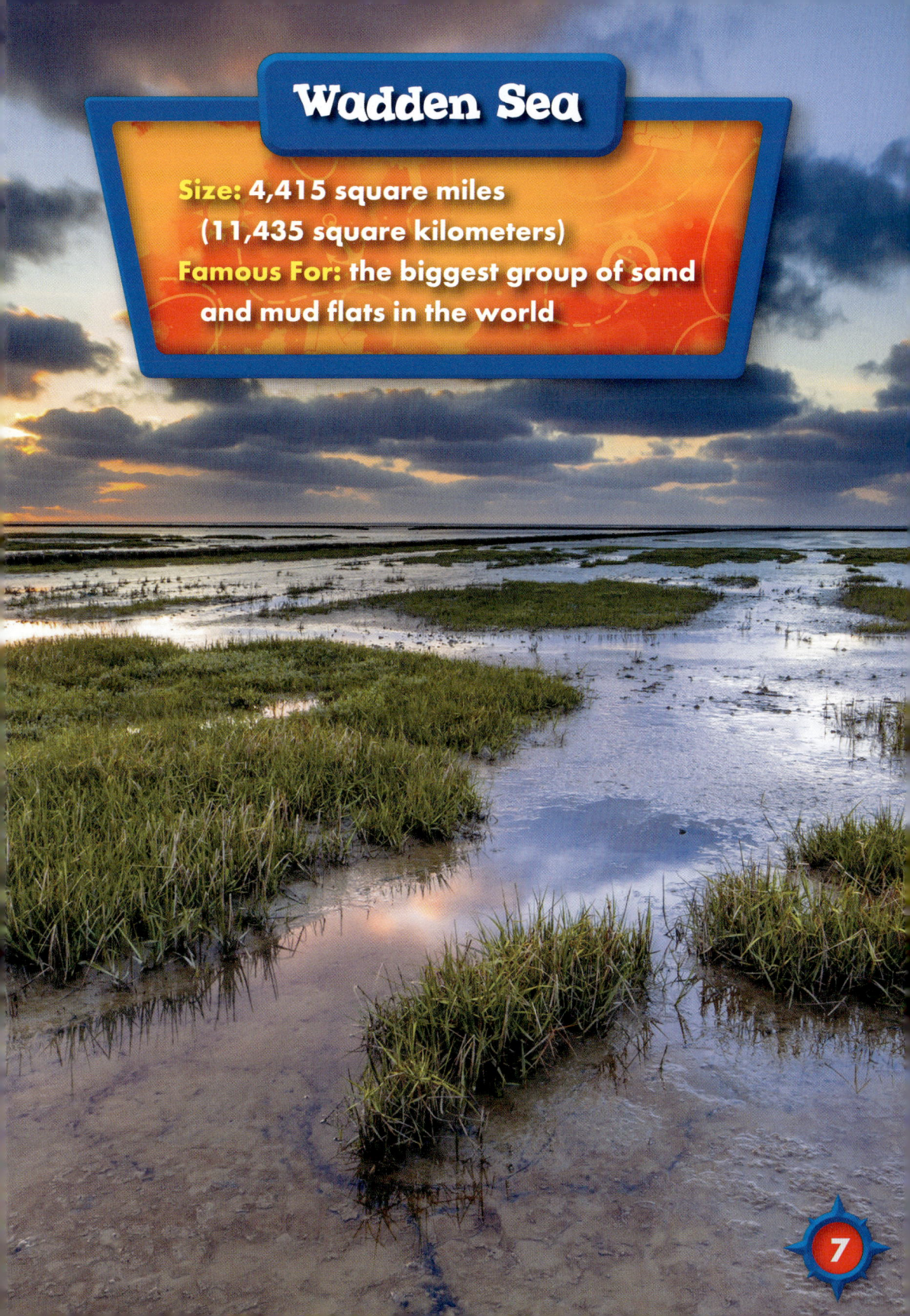

Wadden Sea

Size: 4,415 square miles (11,435 square kilometers)

Famous For: the biggest group of sand and mud flats in the world

The **climate** of the Netherlands is **temperate**. Summers are cool. Winters are cold.

Cloudy skies are common.
It rains often in every season.

Many animals live in the wild. Red deer and badgers live in **reserves**.

Eurasian spoonbill

Animals of the Netherlands

red deer

European badger

Eurasian spoonbill

gray seal

Spoonbills walk through **marshes**. Seals lie in the sun.

Life in the Netherlands

Most people in the Netherlands are Dutch. The country welcomes **immigrants**. Dutch is the main language.

Most people live in cities. The biggest city is Amsterdam.

soccer

ice skating

Soccer is a popular sport. The Dutch love to ride bicycles and ice skate.

Many famous artists have called the country home.

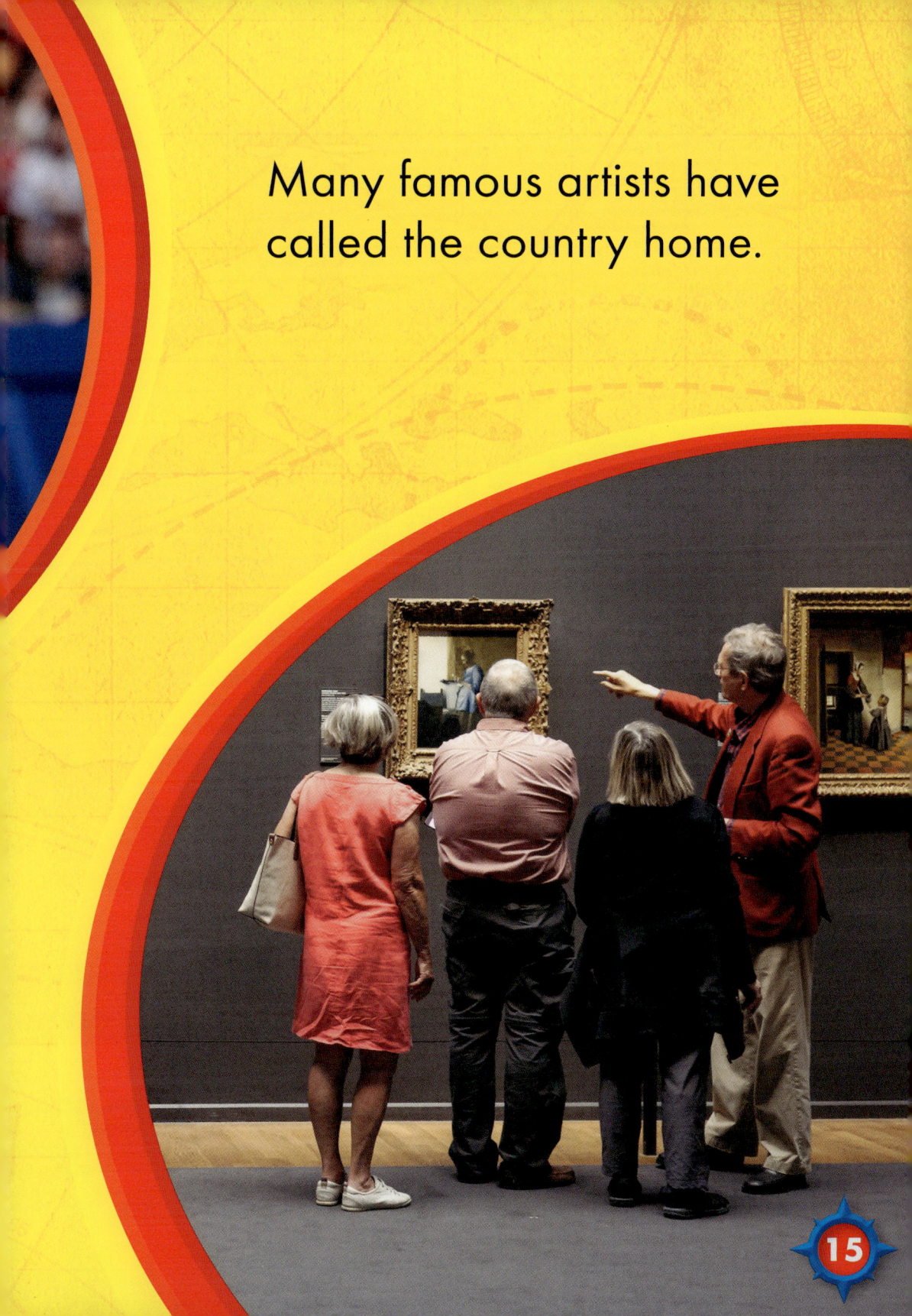

Stamppot is a Dutch dinner. It has mashed potatoes and vegetables. Herring is a favorite seafood.

Dutch Foods

stamppot

herring

gouda

stroopwafels

stroopwafel

Gouda is a popular cheese. *Stroopwafels* are filled with syrup!

King's Day

King's Day honors the country's **monarch**. People visit outdoor markets and festivals.

May 5 is Liberation Day.
People enjoy parades and concerts.
The Dutch love their country!

Netherlands Facts

Size:
16,040 square miles (41,543 square kilometers)

Population:
17,772,378 (2024)

National Holiday:
King's Day (April 27 or April 26)

Main Language:
Dutch

Capital City:
Amsterdam

Famous Face

Name: Karolien Florijn

Famous For: Olympic gold medalist in rowing

Religions

- other: 6%
- Muslim: 5%
- Christian: 35%
- none: 54%

Top Landmarks

Amsterdam Canal District

Anne Frank House

Kinderdijk Windmills

Glossary

canals—waterways that connect to a lake

climate—the usual weather conditions in a certain place

dikes—banks of earth made to control water

immigrants—people who move from one country to another

marshes—low, wet lands

monarch—a person who rules a kingdom

plains—areas of flat land with few trees

reserves—areas of land set aside for wild animals

temperate—related to weather that is not too hot or too cold

To Learn More

AT THE LIBRARY

Kenney, Karen Latchana. *Prairies*. Minneapolis, Minn.: Bellwether Media, 2022.

Mather, Charis. *A Visit to the Netherlands*. Minneapolis, Minn.: Bearport Publishing, 2023.

Spanier, Kristine. *Netherlands*. Minneapolis, Minn.: Jump!, 2021.

ON THE WEB

FACTSURFER

Factsurfer.com gives you a safe, fun way to find more information.

1. Go to www.factsurfer.com.
2. Enter "the Netherlands" into the search box and click 🔍.
3. Select your book cover to see a list of related content.

Index

Amsterdam, 4, 5, 12
animals, 10, 11
artists, 15
bike, 14
canals, 6
capital (see Amsterdam)
climate, 8
coast, 6
dams, 6
dikes, 6
Dutch, 12
Europe, 4
flooding, 6
food, 16, 17
ice skate, 14
King's Day, 18
Liberation Day, 19
map, 5
marshes, 11
mud flats, 6, 7

Netherlands facts, 20–21
people, 12, 14, 15, 18, 19
plains, 6
rain, 9
reserves, 10
say hello, 13
soccer, 14
summers, 8
Wadden Sea, 7
winters, 8

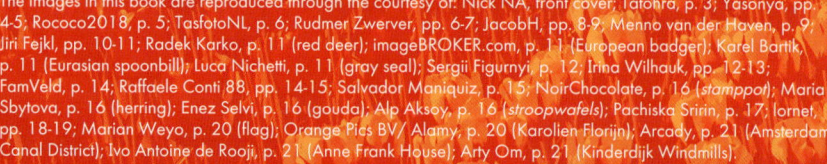

The images in this book are reproduced through the courtesy of: Nick NA, front cover; Tatohra, p. 3; Yasonya, pp. 4-5; Rococo2018, p. 5; TasfotoNL, p. 6; Rudmer Zwerver, pp. 6-7; JacobH, pp. 8-9; Menno van der Haven, p. 9; Jiri Fejkl, pp. 10-11; Radek Karko, p. 11 (red deer); imageBROKER.com, p. 11 (European badger); Karel Bartik, p. 11 (Eurasian spoonbill); Luca Nichetti, p. 11 (gray seal); Sergii Figurnyi, p. 12; Irina Wilhauk, pp. 12-13; FamVeld, p. 14; Raffaele Conti 88, pp. 14-15; Salvador Maniquiz, p. 15; NoirChocolate, p. 16 (*stamppot*); Maria Sbytova, p. 16 (herring); Enez Selvi, p. 16 (gouda); Alp Aksoy, p. 16 (*stroopwafels*); Pachiska Sririn, p. 17; lornet, pp. 18-19; Marian Weyo, p. 20 (flag); Orange Pies BV/ Alamy, p. 20 (Karolien Florijn); Arcady, p. 21 (Amsterdam Canal District); Ivo Antoine de Rooji, p. 21 (Anne Frank House); Arty Om, p. 21 (Kinderdijk Windmills).